Border Security

Bruce Dawe

Bruce Dawe's poetry has been taught in schools and universities for over forty years and he is Australia's best-selling living poet. Born in Melbourne in 1930 he left school early and worked in various positions before joining the RAAF in 1958 where he served for nine years including six months in Malaysia. He began teaching in 1969 at Downlands College in Toowoomba then lectured at DDIAE/USQ until retiring in 1993. He continues to teach several literature classes a week through the University of the Third Age. He completed all his degrees, a B.A., Litt.B., M.A., and Ph.D. by part-time study.

Bruce Dawe
Border
Security
and other poems

U W
A P
Poetry

First published in 2016 by
UWA Publishing
Crawley, Western Australia 6009
www.uwap.uwa.edu.au

UWAP is an imprint of UWA Publishing
a division of The University of Western Australia

THE UNIVERSITY OF
**WESTERN
AUSTRALIA**

National Library of Australia
Cataloguing-in-Publication entry:
Dawe, Bruce, 1930– author.
Border security / Bruce Dawe.
ISBN: 9781742589138 (paperback)
Australian poetry.
A821.3

Designed by Becky Chilcott, Chil3
Typeset in Lyon Text by Lasertype
Printed by Lightning Source

This project has been assisted by the Australian
Government through the Australia Council, its arts
funding and advisory body.

Australian Government | Australia
Council
for the Arts

uwapublishing

For my children,
Brian, Jamie, Katrina, and Melissa

with love

And also
my deepest appreciation
to Brian Musgrove, whose
invaluable assistance made this
selection possible...
And to Mary Coffey
for all her typing...

Some of the poems in this collection have
previously appeared in the following publications:

AD 2000
Canberra Times
Cordite Poetry Review
Courier-Mail
Idiom
Island
Madonna
Meanjin
Quadrant
Quarterly Voice
Southerly
ULM Press
The Australian
The Mozzie
Westerly

Contents

Suburbanites All...

in this Clay suburb to abide
Rubaiyat of Omar Khayyam
trans. Edward Fitzgerald

Wherever and however in *this* suburb
Each of us, by definition, lives
Sooner or later something of the experience
Will account for the occasional negatives.
Whether it's so often with a feeling
That a TO LET sign somehow has been placed
On that particular lot which is existence.
For some it's with a marked degree of haste
From early occupancy, while elsewhere
That sign gets hammered in by ill-health, age,
Or accidents 'waiting to happen', which then *did*.
Omar has warned us, page after page,
That this temporary bit of real-estate that's ours,
Bourgeois or buggered, plush or penurious, that we've got
For all our fond illusioning of powers
Can never be passed on.   This temporary lot
In the nature of things weeded or run to seed, bright
With the latest doodads (like Dr Edelsten's Gwynne)
Will only exist in the things which made it ours,
Whether it was good or bad, for living in.

Pro Bono

for Barney Cooney

For me you have always been
the epitome of good humour
– seeing you there, waiting
with the air hostess
as the last passenger on Flight 837 (me)
approached the departure gate,
you were still that genial
person you always were, *back when,*
and we could as easily have been
at the Newman Society in 1954
or smiling at your remarks as groom
at your wedding – the good-kindliness
the same as then while you sought
in Lygon Street (changed but unchanged)
a parking-spot and a place for a snack.
We need increasingly such natural
bonhomie, not learned in some latter-day
Dale Carnegie seminar, but rising instead
from original springs of the spirit
we can never afford to forget
– thank you for reminding me once again.

Measureless

Often, when not sure how long the journey
Nor when we will return, we pause and smile,
The time, the distance troubling us, we say:
'We'll be away awhile...'

'A while' may be some years, some months, some days
(Definitions defeat us when the heart's
Caught up in happening's omnipresent web,
Still fluttering for release as hope departs).

But still by every means we seek to soothe
Awareness of that unavoidable choice,
Confronting us and those we love,
And in a carefully firm and gentle voice,

That memorable re-assurance treasured
When life and after-life we reconcile
In words as memorably echoing as a bell:
'We'll be away awhile...'

Strange

for Raffaella Torresān

For the very young everything is strange
Even before they can pronounce the word
(Or spell it); comforts and terrors come,
And puzzlement is always within range:
The carolling of some early-morning bird,
The noises that tap (or beat) upon the drum
Of consciousness, the growing dawn and dark,
The rain, the human voices near and far, the stark
Hungers and thirsts – what can they mean
When mornings shuffle past in blurred
Succession, or crowd around with murmuring voices?
Who can explain the sun, the stars, the moon,
Or time, that ever-mysterious medium
Through which the world of phenomena appear and disappear?

And yet even the not-so-young
May be forgiven if, at times, it seems
Worlds within worlds (present, future, past)
Collide as they do in dreams...
In the supermarkets of the universe
We roller-skate at speeds too fast
To assess the value of anything except the price
Of roller skates (or at least, the last
Price when we bought the present wobbly pair).
In the expanding aisles we hurtle through,
Let's take time out from visiting the nearest zoo
– Is anything more 'strange' than *me* – and *you*?

Mini-series

mais qui voit la fleur, dont voir le soleil

Dawn, clock-face of the heavens, becomes
momentous with fulfilment, birds
with the eccentricity of minutes, wake,
launch themselves into the unfolding
air of time, each with its own beady
reading of history: insects too
stir into action and that same air
in its bland magnanimity, takes them in
as the cash-converters down below
open their everlasting doors to the latest
needful – the world at large is ready for
business: early ants carting home
the injured and the accidentally dead,
young magpies squawking for
another handout and the heart
punching the body's bundy only yet
half-awake to what may come
down the chute to it before
the next night signs it off.

Reasons

'We'd go more often, mind you, but, you know,
How kids are in hospital, when they're sick:
They cry when you first come, and when you go
(Their little faces streaked with woe)
Tend to make your hospital visits *quick*.

It's the same now (only different) when you've brought
Poor old Mum or Dad or Aunty Jane
To some far nursing-home (the last resort)
Among those ghostly others who've been caught
By age and incapacity and pain...

So, who can blame us if we then decide
It's cruel to remind them of the world
And how it was (and *is* for us, still) there, outside,
Flapping with possibilities, while theirs died,
Forgotten like flags that are forever furled?

No, much as we'd like to visit, let's be frank
And agree that, looked at *realistically*,
In the long run they wouldn't thank
Us for reminding them that their life sank
The day we launched them on this final silent sea.'

Evening Wolves

'evening wolves, that leave nothing till the morning...'
Zephaniah 3:3

As the sun sinks from the sky
and the shadows close in
as the birds begin to seek
their evening nests,
and the frail and elderly
(who sometimes feel that they
have out-lived their lives)
draw their curtains, thinking
of the loneliness surrounding them
like a wintry landscape.

Then it is that certain creatures
emerge from anonymous urban forests,
their keen senses hungering for
those carefully garnered savings
so, now they come:
pointing out the rusty guttering,
the battered cladding and the peeling
paintwork, the leaking ceiling, the cracked
pathway, and those missing palings and even appear busy
for some moments before departing
(often with the money in advance)
back into the forests, never to be
seen again, leaving as a legacy
of their pitiless visits
the broken sound of sobbing.

Peace

for Liz

You pass on the peace that you have found
    (or, rather, have been *given*)
stronger than any ore in earthly ground,
    being forged in Heaven...

Those who know you soon discover why
    they too are drawn
into the circumambience of that sky,
    that loving dawn.

The world at large does not always present
    its loveliest face,
while you like a faithful and beneficent
    sun, bestow your grace

On all you meet. I know, as one whose heart
    has darker seasons,
I, too, have been blessed, from the very start,
    by your sweet reasons.

So often, too, I've seen, in other's eyes,
    that certain good
which walks where you walk, lightening the skies
    and the darkling wood...

Conjunctions

We are continually subject to conjunctions:
a friend of ours becomes a handsome emissary
between the place where Liz and I first met and loved
(after my first wife's death)
and where we live now. She rolls up
in a BMW sports (borrowed) to collect
a three-foot high lemon tree grown here
to give to her sister living in Toowoomba. As she drives off,
waving (the lemon tree with four ripe lemons on it
swaying in the breeze of her departure; we wave back, smiling
at her front seat passenger swathed in a sheet,
still nodding yellow). And I feel
I've given back a peculiar sweetness
to that upland city where I spent
some thirty years most profitably, but with that usual
fruit of sadnesses as well, some still lacking
resolution. If only we could send *them* off as cheerfully
as this extremely modest citrus offering. But then,
such conjunctions are so clearly written into
the grammar of our living, anyway...

On the Opening of the Albury Library Museum

27th July 2007

Here in this place both past and future meet
And in the living present join their power,
Just as in every marriage that's replete
There lies a richness which transcends the hour
And makes it memorable for years to come.
– So time will add its own encomium...

Here learning and research will jointly try
The work (*and* pleasure) of discovery
– And, as in successful weddings, justify
The planning, the expenditure which will see
The region's many hopes and dreams expand
To add to its renown throughout the land,
And, as a living river at our door,
Make friends of those who come, forevermore.

Visiting a High-Care Centre

We are born in a clearing, but we die in a forest.
Russian proverb

There are those who never speak
  and those who never speak to strangers

There is the man who cries loudly *Hello* into a cushion he
  carries around with him (and occasionally *Help*)

There are the ones who appear to be sound asleep
  and whose legs and feet have to be bandaged

There are those who shuffle around in their walking-frames

And those who merely sit

And those who have to be spoon-fed

In this general community area there is a buzz of activity
  like the confused overlapping sound of innumerable bees
    whose honey is not of this world and whose many languages
      suggest a mysterious garden where carers are attentive
        to a bewildering wilderness of necessities,
          moving among the chairs and arm-chairs
            with words and actions of comfort

There are others who are here only because their legs are no longer
  strong enough to enable them to be at home

This world too is another word for 'forest'.

The Auction

Sometimes it seems we were brought here only to mourn
That all our happiness, our future plans,
Are fruits of the salesmen's lure to 'get us in',
To have us bid more eagerly in an auction
Which, despite the glowing ads, the *bonhomie*
Of the agents and the boisterous auctioneer,
We will, in due course, find ourselves lamenting:
'This fabulous dwelling! Those rooms, the views!'
Appear as mocking echoes to us as we finally drive away,
Outbid by younger buyers...
                                  It's then we feel
Regret for ever daring, *once*, to suppose
We could out-bid futurity and stay
Forever in this mansion made of clay.

Eating Voices

'Whenever it is you eat us
You also eat our voices,
The terror that we're feeling,
Our desperate lack of choices,
Our fright when we are freighted
And headed for extinction,
The smell of death that greets us
Each time without distinction...
Where once were grass and fodder
Or, at least, feed-lots, and water,
Soon or late we're driven
Afar from these, to slaughter;
You'll see it in our staring
Eyes that view the distance
Which separates us finally
From what was our existence...
That happy animal heaven
(Which is *your* childhood's blessing)
Has nothing with that later
Hell *you'd* find distressing.

The blood, the screams, the woeful
Struggles terribly ended
With your own childhood memories
Cannot be nicely blended.
Your merriment, rejoicing
At art's fond transformations,
Cannot take away from us
Our smothered lamentations.

Tears cannot bridge the chasm,
Nor sentiment altogether
Stifle the sounds of suffering
We bring in *every* weather.

Vast industries abound wherein
Brute death meets appetite,
Though our voices in some distant dream
May haunt you at first light.'

Taking Care

'Take care...' We often say these words
Along with our goodbyes,
And 'taking care' by visiting
Is eminently wise,
Care is a special sacrament
We all both *need* and *give;*
It lights our lives as well as those
Amongst whom we must live,
Each care-giver, then, takes on
A priestly role, no less
Beneficent than those, indeed
Whose presence is to bless.
It is the bread and wine of hearts
And minds that everywhere,
In all the realms of need, extend
That providential prayer
Which says, in every instance:
'We're here, take comfort, then,
And should you need more comfort, why,
We'll hasten back again!'

Tribute

for Ken

Wisdom and care with you walked always together.
– I cannot think of you now in any other way;
There was never in my mind any question as to whether
What you *did* was one thing, another what you might *say*...

That kindness which springs from loving consideration
Still animates you now, as it did your scholarly frame.
– I still haven't found in thirty years' confabulation
The least diminution of the many things I could name!

Without you, my world (and that of so many others)
Would have been infinitely poorer, just as the air
We breathe is too often taken for granted (familiarity smothers
Gifts that would be bitterly missed if no longer there).

I have often despaired at even beginning
To do justice to all that you've meant to me through the years
But not to attempt to, at least, would be the greater sinning,
Such inarticulacy being (like *The King's Speech*) one of my fears,

So here, for what it is worth, in spite of my stammering,
Is the thanks I can never reduce to a quatrain of words,
That inward thanks which defies all outward clamouring,
And is perhaps best left, after all, to more heavenly birds...

Hearts and Flowers

for Liz

Flowers have no trumpets at their coming,
No ritual pomp and ceremony to declare
The beauty which they bring, no army's drumming
To thunder their uniqueness to the air...

Some flowers are winter visitors appearing
(Like some family members who will steer
Towards us when we find less cause for cheering
And the elements are otherwise chill and drear).

But, come what may, each season has its blessing,
And buds obey the nature of their kind.
While we, with science, try to keep nature guessing,
That motherly soul has other things in mind.

So, in the gardens of our daily living,
Good deeds, like flowers, aren't always based upon
Ceremonies to reward us in our giving,
Like flower-shows on which the world's sun shone,

For each of us should wear (as inspiration)
The flowers of others' giving, as a spur
To nurturing in year-long cultivation,
All the flowers that *can* be, and that ever *were*...

Late Admission

If I could have been a better father
I think I would have been, but the blue-print
Got shoved away in a drawer somewhere
And when it came time to use it I couldn't find it,
The real-estate men were at the door,
A *FOR SALE* hammered into the front lawn,
And the phone kept ringing even when I'd left it off the hook.
So what was I to do but go on pretending
That everything was under control when it clearly wasn't:
The garden neglected, nothing sorted out
And no place even to go, the removalist's van
Already patiently waiting in our short street,
And a number of grandchildren I rarely get to see
Vaguely waving goodbye?!

The Beatitudes

Matthew 5

Not pious words of what's to be,
Not a vision of what's to come,
But as a *present* possibility
That sermon, like a drum,
Summons us from where we *are*
To blessedness here and now,
Through all the vicissitudes that scar,
The pain that bids us bow,
The tyranny of great and small,
Greed's vast impoverishment,
The losses that afflict us all,
The happiness only lent...

Those words of Jesus still acclaim
(For *that* world, and for *this*)
That the deepest joys which He can name,
The only permanent bliss,
Belong to those whose hungry care
Is for righteousness as for bread,
With those who are merciful and forebear
Giving 'sweet revenge' its head,
With the pure in heart and those whose love
Of God is not denied
By a love of self which soars above
All godliness in pride...
True peace, He promised, is that state
Whose reality must start
Not in the councils of the great
But in the human heart.

Two thousand years have not made less
The beatitudes' lasting claim
On those who through such blessedness
Have honoured His great name.

Here...

Psalm 37 reconsidered

In this friendly foreign country
our history no longer exists
while theirs is ever-present to them,
the anecdotes of memory possess
continual resonance and the scenes
from many childhoods are replayed
on festive occasions from the spools
of the past. In Babylon
we are between our fading recollections
of Zion and the two great rivers
of death and forgetting (which is another
shorter death). These psalms we hold
to our hearts like harps, but usefulness
is denied us by definition, and the ziggurats
of alien gods remain
as reminders of our exile.

Cardiologist

to O. Henry

You've taken the city's beating ambivalent heart
(your metaphors your gloves)
and kept it alive with witty electric wires
while in your hands still pulsing with its loves,
sutured its many rhythms and arrhythmia with due care
(with humorous asides to us, your attentive theatre staff
so that, we, too, even though gowned and masked, share
and find time to laugh),
for, whatever burg your patients hearken from
we still breathe easy, since we know
wry-eyed wisdom guides those surgeon's hands
as they glide to and fro
from the depths of the Bowery to Manhattan, from Fifth
Avenue to Brickdust Row.

Il Silenzio

After my first wife's death,
I often used to play a taped recording
of a trumpet solo called *Il Silenzio*.
It said a lot to me then that I still believe:
that everyone goes into the great silence
(the good, the bad, the indifferent),
and these days it is as loud as the Last Post
at six o'clock on an RSL evening,
holding up for recollection
the phlegmatic action of time
which heralds in advance our own dissolution
in the returning fragments of those lives
and loved creatures which speak to us often
by their absence. At times, that keening silence
drowns out what others, in the passing
present, are murmuring, so that,
however hard one tries,
one cannot hear them.

For Maureen Freer

Friends meet and part and often,
According to the many works and days
That come between and soften
The edges of voyaging, their separate ways
Blur memory's particulars, and yet
It only takes a meeting and a book-
Launch to help us to forget
How much of time has gone...
                              Why, look,
Meeting you in the Red Room brought so much
Of the seventies and the eighties back that I'm
Not surprised that the latest touch
Can be as immediate as it ever was in time
Long past... Rest assured: if remembering
Can be some comfort, then being linked to
Our prayers in present days, it's one more thing
Joining us to the many friends you've made, near and far,
Whose light revisits us like that evening star.

We poets know we have to tend *our* land
As conscientiously as farmers (for good reason);
Your whole life has seen 'a real good harvest', and
I was honoured, in one recent Brisbane season,
To help bring in a literary crop (no cow
Got bogged; indoors, no fear of rain),
You'd already cleared the brigalow and driven the plough,
And, if called on, I'm sure you would do it again!

Dawn Scene

This other daybreak and these other clouds
move on the steely mirror of the lake
with annotations by an early gull
or cormorant... beyond this plagiarism
real clouds, real sky, real birds, the unseen sun
adds its illuminating commentary; now the lake
frowns at the thought of winds, a delicate multiple
questioning of the process; farther off
light on the water is a turbulent flickering as though
an eager school of silver fingerlings had gathered
to learn the epistemology of the day.

A Late Word from Hughie

His Christianity is a social gospel...Taking Christ
as an example should make people 'good blokes'...
while God is better thought of as Hughie.

Peter Kuch

'Well I know it's pretty hard to believe it now
but I had things all worked out for that little place: the dam
right there the house just over by the peppercorns
a good big belt of timber for the native bears
and all the other animals as well as a good-size billabong
for the water-birds paddocks begging to be ploughed and planted
oh and a nice stretch of river for the fish and last but not least
a family to be proud of beginning of course with a son
and I got one right out of this world just couldn't
ever do enough for his old man did things you'd hardly believe
if I told you I meant to leave the place to him y'know
when the time came couldn't have ever been in safer hands but well
the best-laid plans I still blame those big-city lawyers meself
and their damned paper-work in next to no time they were swarming
all over the place I looked in one day shortly after I left
and I simply couldn't recognize the old homestead what happened
I said to my boy and he said I'm sorry Dad I tried to keep 'em out
but there were so many of 'em I didn't stand a chance
– so we packed up there and then and moved to another universe
you probably haven't heard of yet but mind you I still get the odd call
to replenish the water-supply for some cockie who's just about droughted
out
still it's a far cry from how it used to be in the old days
so even if they asked me to take the whole farm off their hands
it's mortgaged to the hilt now y'know and of course
I'd have to talk to my boy about it after all he's been through
I don't know if I'd be happy to take that risk again.'

The Cup and the Lip

a defining moment in a Swans–Bomber AFL game

Having marked 50 yards out
with the game in the balance
(your team having come back from
a potentially devastating defeat
to the very brink of victory),
you could have taken your time
and had your kick for a possible winning goal
but moved to play on and, in that tiny fragment of time,
lost what you stood to win; the umpire waved his hand
and the game was over...

                                              Our lives are made up
of such momentary decisions
between the imponderable choices we make
and the unforeseen consequences
which follow – with the great crowd
of red-and-black rising to greet
the seemingly certain success
and the red-and-white warriors recovering from
the cliff's-edge of defeat
to suddenly find victory, after all,
expressing the indulgent mandate of heaven.

Dog Heaven

for Susan Johnson

Presently, there's Suzi,
part Maltese terrier, part Lhasa Apso (from *4 Paws*)
for whom we discovered this beach at Currimundi,
known locally as Dog Heaven where dog-lovers by the dozen
take their four-legged friends off-leash – as close
as dogs can get to a heavenly state of being,
while still earth-bound... It's a revelation
to see them greet each other in amity, dance around,
then race flat-out together (as little kids do,
for the sheer fun of it) peeling off, then,
in long and joyous bursts, when not
applying their superbly visionary noses
to whatever the tide serves up. Oh yes, if we
(so busy nowadays declaring heaven either
out-of-bounds or a sham) could only find
our own endless beach, the one we share, at times,
when such untethered intervals are offered,
the world would surely be
a better, safer place: for *us*, for *them!*
Sometimes at night I seem to hear
dream-barking.

May the Forceps be with You.

Whenever I get out a crime novel from the local library
I also get out my tweezers, ready for whatever
forensic evidence comes my way from previous readers...
It's the *guys* mostly who leave the clues of their interest
all over the pages: the tobacco-shreds, the cigarette ash,
the food-particles, the suspicious stains that are usually
grubby fingers. Sometimes there are even pedantic corrections
to American spellings or idiomatic expressions unknown
to numbnuts still catching up on their secondary schooling.

But who has the time to match up their calligraphy
with the signatures of approval on the fly-leaf, or at least
a low-browed and defining presence, like that
of contemporary visitors intent on improving
ancient aboriginal rock art?

I'm not one of your out-of-work gumshoes, mind you,
but the opening is there for some dedicated private eye
to set up in a battered office in the Bronx
(or Footscray, for that matter) just to track down
some of these perps. I'm afraid I've got too many
other cases to ever compete with Sam Spade or Mike Hammer.
And, anyway, my natural curiosity doesn't reach that far.

Entomology I

Sometimes the eyes are flies,
crawling over one's face, hands,
clothes. Feeding busily, but ever-ready
for vertical take-off if challenged,
– disappearing back into the heads they came from
bearing their own special-interest food in the form
of messages to that multi-channelled receptacle:
the brain. These eyes seek all forms of nourishment
the mind and heart demand: the sweet essences
of love, infatuation, admiration, care, distilled
by each of us and sought by each of us, while only
too aware of the potential presence of
insecticides designed to discourage
such intrusions into our space. It is impossible
to know (or even be vaguely aware of) all
the benefits and/or harm such insectival life
may bring to us, or others. The Nos may have
their own particular obligations in the parliament
of the atmosphere, but it's usually the Ayes
that most often spell out the future
for most of us, whether we like it or not.

Popping the Question

for Liz

On our very first date, while driving,
out of the blue dusk you asked me
a question which mythical creatures
such as the Sphinx might have sprung on
wary mortals: 'Which is more important:
kindness or intelligence?' Not being
either Oedipus or even Stephen Fry
I saw the entire prospect of romance
shrivelling in the passenger-seat before
it even got started, but I knew
that I had to come up with an answer
no later than immediately and that
like any exam student faced with a serious
invigilator I realised I would be unable to
plead for extra time.
                          Every serious question
since then from that same source has in it
something of the surprise and shock of
that first one, but unlike the examinees
of legend (even were my failing hearing
not a compounding factor) I am usually unable
to come up with as satisfactory an answer
as I did that first mythical time, when,
like Theseus I was provided with a single
thread of wit to guide me through the maze.

Companions

Although none of them will ever make it
to any awards ceremonies, these little
moths which are my companions of the bath
fascinate me; they are surely in some
mothologist's manual flying out with
eye-blinks of modest greeting to such keen
students as seek them there, but for me
they are like the minuscule brown ants
which suddenly happen upon your page
while reading: visible reminders of
life-forms playing for good or evil
or devil-may-care their parts in that
perennial parade which move before us
and within us often in secret labs
seeking to outwit our latest stratagems
but to these showering companions I feel
obliged to give my daily nod of acknowledgement.

Friends

A faithful friend is the medicine of life.
Ecclesiastes

for Gell
who is blessed with many such friends

As from a deep well at night
we see the stars
even more brightly than elsewhere, their light
more keenly seen,
so, in our darkest times, our inward sight
(which daylight mars)
helps us to realize more clearly then
the constancy of those whose love
has always been
a constellation circling above
as faithfully as that sun whose influence
on them in turn bestows
unblinking beneficence...

Among Those Missing

I was never there when any of them died:
my mother, my father, my sisters, my brother,
close friends, other loved ones – I was always
somewhere else (not on purpose, mind you,
but still, I often think about this, just the same...).
The death-bed scene was written into our parents'
Victorian sensibilities, a focal point
for future mourning, but it so happens
I was always among the missing;
for me, the last time was always some time *before*,
so that the final looks, the final gestures, the words
often memorialized in a nation's fiction
as well as in the unforgettable facts,
were never ever there
for me to hold up in memory's glass
as a poignant toast at the point of departure,

the chevrons of service denied,
the Last Post just out of earshot.

Caring

an appreciation of my experience as a patient
at Sunshine Coast Private Hospital, August 2008

How do we sum up just how much we owe
To those who care for us when we are down,
When nights are long and days just come and go
And the sick body bids the spirit frown?

There is no calculus can assess the sum
We owe to those we meet at such a time:
Surgeon, anaesthetist, theatre staff – all come
To help the body's faltering prose to rhyme...

Back from that battle front, we're wheeled to where
Other nurses, like ministering angels, wait
To add their often intravenous care
We're not always conscious of, until (too late!)
We're fully dressed again, and on our way
Back to that world we left with trembling shanks
So long (or short) ago, too precipitately to say
That voluble and all-too-inadequate thanks
We tender *now*:
                  for every smile and healing touch.

A Bit of a Breeze

Living here on the coast is usually a bit of a breeze,
almost every day it whispers from the sea,
cooling, refreshing, the very breath of heaven,
but when big storm rains came in suddenly
we were taken by surprise,
and I was amazed to hear next door's
visiting children playing happily in it
at night, and so I thought: *Good luck to them!*
But how do they manage to do it in this weather?!
It wasn't until I opened the window and the storm-children
rushed in squealing and laughing
that I recognized whose children *these* were.

Employment Problem

Of course, I shouldn't have been employing them
on an early morning shift, anyway
(my legs, I mean). So when I fell
twice on that concrete footpath just down the road,
fracturing my skull and an eye-socket
and breaking my nose, I was already feeling
a bit off (pneumonia, as it turns out), and where
I usually had *legs* there were, suddenly, just these two
strips of shredded paper and so down I went, head-first.
Two large pools of blood marked my falls, but
I can't get over my *legs*, those fairly reliable
workmen, just giving up on me, as if I was
a crooked employer they had suddenly decided
to walk out on, leaving me scrabbling to
make sense of it, after all those years of mutually gainful
industry!
            They're back again, now, looking
dutiful and subservient, hoping for their
old jobs back... But (one bruised brow still
raised in doubt) I don't know whether
I can trust them. These skinned knuckles, knee-caps,
finger-tips, and torn tendon are like
reminders of the oil-rags and worn
playing-cards those workmen left behind
when they just up and walked off the job
early that Monday morning... Still,
I know I'm a softie, so: 'Ok, fellers,
but this is your *last chance*, right?'

The God of Thumbs

For the god of thumbs at last I've learned
a proper respect
– learned through one's sudden
incapacity how much I can expect
of every artificer
in the body-shop
including those pugnacious
little characters who cop
so much of the blame should
anything go wrong
– oh sure, thumbs are meant to be
the dominant ever-so-strong
band-leaders in the quintet,
or a Roman emperor giving
the Yea or Nay to gladiator fingers
for their affirmative living
but Hey they say think of us rather
as part of the whole big ball of wax
subject when malfunctioning
to unsympathetic
public attacks
– bandaged and wired up
I will never be quite the same
as when I was (previously uninjured)
a part of the game;
hence this belated thanks in a way
to the god of thumbs
for this latest update on our mutual vulnerability
however *unintentionally* it comes.

Border Security

'Have you anything to declare?' they always ask,
And while, in all good conscience, we say, 'No...'
At times we're the first to take ourselves to task
And, being officially cleared, may straightway go
To that other customs desk that's set within,
Where officers, accustomed to the lies
Expediency urges on us, will begin
To go through all our luggage while each tries
To explain it all away: the forbidden fruit
The ornamental weapons never meant
For violent use, of course, and the medication
That could just be 'prohibited'.
                                How readily bent
Is often the offence to the occasion.
Meanwhile we travellers traduce ourselves to stand,
Innocent passports in each trembling hand.

Walking Our Dog

To know no more of nights and days
puzzles me still,
like the child who (perforce) in the cupboard lays
those toys and contrivances that still
are dear to him, however much
they've also meant to others who before
his time (O long before!) had loved to touch,
to hold and treasure.
Walking our dog (the latest
of that family I've known) for many a measure
I think of those others who
survived it all, and in turn left
it all behind, just as we, too,
must leave, some sooner and some late,
as though the mother of all life should come
and '*Tchk, tchk*' say, 'Why, look, it's after eight,
and past your bed-time... Come,
put all those playthings by... That's right!',
then tuck you in for that last sleep
and that longest most mysterious night...

Noah Redivivus

Queensland Floods

And if in their public utterances
their voices are often choked
it's with the débris of their lives
as the floodwaters ravage them,
sweeping away the household minutiae
as well as the bulkier things, the photos
framing a life-time, and the frail walls
that witnessed so much... 'What can you do?'
some wonder, their imaginations dazed
by the new spaces and rubble
as unsympathetic as rent-collectors
who have called at the wrong time
when you have no explanation that will excuse
your sudden poverty and unpreparedness. But then, suddenly
come those others awakened
like a counter-flood, saying *Well, we couldn't just stand there;*
we had to do what we could, right?
– the human *urgency* called upon to meet
the desperately human *need*.

South-south-west of Sorrow

'South-south-west of sorrow
Lay that land,
For which we gave up everything
But breath;
What else were we to do,
For whom the north
Meant persecution, misery,
And death?
Even so, the maps they gave us
And the charts
Belied the swivelling compass
Of our hearts...
So, every sunrise
Like a troubled beast,
Frowned down upon us
From the heaving east,
And every wave that
Cheated us of rest
Was matched by the watchful tumult
In each breast...
Now, here, in this placid south-land
We must wait
Once more upon the vicissitudes
Of fate.'

Recapitulation

for Liz

As I had no option then,
so I have none now;
you were there to be loved,
and I felt, somehow,
that if I could only find some way
to bend, to scrape, to bow,
though stammering, I might turn
my 'I' into a 'Thou'...
The task will never be done... For now,
whenever it seems
that sometimes, late at night,
encouraged by dreams,
when the inquisitorial sun
has gone and the bland moon beams,
and the words beyond words there in my head
have dwindled from reams
to meandering rivulets,
impoverished streams.
There never will be, for me,
sufficient time
to find in the forests of prose,
or on the hills of rhyme,
in age's Antarctic snows,
or in a more temperate clime,
in metaphor, image, or symbol,
an effective paradigm
to encompass all that I feel,
thinking of you
let it ensue,

that whatever I once felt of love
(extravagantly, it's true)
is what, in these time-worn lines,
I *still* feel, too.

Considering Clouds on a Sunday Morning

As thoughtful as the day is
when its brow is clouded as though
it were back in school and the sum on the blackboard
is a difficult one or like an air apparent
still to decide whether to reign or not; often
the trees hang listless waiting for
the big decision as though the moment
is something they have to put up with, their leafy
crowds subject to the downpour, the drizzle
as if either were just what they wanted.
And still the clouds move at their own
overwhelming pace, their progress
beyond most of us who are not meteorologists
or farmers, being simply those over whom
the clouds rule in their own deliberate
authoritarian way. Some of course have tried
shooting them but it does not always seem
to solve the problem. They are above us
and we know (although we try not to think about it)
that they can turn nasty or even radio-active
at any time.

Jig-Saw

We find the jig-saw working out, piece by piece:
(This bit of sky...that bit of muddy ground...
And – over here – a corner of a castle),
– We cannot know the whole scene at this moment,
But what we have determines us to find
More bits for filling in the space between.
We try to match each unknown to the known
(Sometimes we're right – encouragement enough
For us to go on eagerly sorting through
The random pieces, searching for that one
Designed to add its colour, shape, and meaning
To what's already there...).
                              We each, I think,
Hold in our hearts a guesstimate of what
We imagine was the whole kit when it came
From the Game-maker who must surely smile
Each time we match up something that we try
To what's already there, saying as we do:
"Ah, yes, *that* fits!"
                        Just as eyes meet and lock,
And hands and arms and bodies in *their* ways
Work at such puzzles, too, so minds contrive
To fill *their* jig-saw in, although this game
Goes on forever; there's no final frame...

Orchid Children

for Liz

Happy Christmas, once again, my dear,
And to your colourful and growing band
Of orchid-children thriving, as we speak.
I've seen them adding to the seasonal cheer,
Responding to your ever-loving hand:
The fully-grown, the very young, the weak,
And witnessed daily how your mothering heart
Tends them as thoroughly as you always do
Your human family... This is the start
Of another adventurous rendezvous for you
And I can see already how they reach
Blossomwards for what you plan to teach
Them, and the world itself be richer for this time
You'll spend with gifts both silent... and sublime.

Anéantissement

A guilt-edged grief! But why
does this one harry me so persistently
that the therapy of inscription
drives me at 5.00 am to tease the riddle out?
I have said goodbye before, though never so precisely
aimed at the event – in this case, a caring vet's
last rites... I think perhaps it's the absences,
now growing ever longer, which cast one's hopeless stroking,
one's desperate farewells in such lugubrious light.
Creatures such as this, thirsting for water, nauseated
by our constant proffering of food, leave such unexpectedly
monumental gaps in one's daily life, it seems
that neither time nor goodly arguments for their willed demise
can ever hope to fill, while the goodbye words
and gestures in themselves seem echoes of deceit:
that this innocent creature should now go
to her reasoned doom to spare her further suffering
in a world where such dooms are the common lot
still haunts as painfully as the world's first.

Loss is the sickening aftermath of loving, and our thanks
as desperate as a dance of midges in a bathroom mirror.
It's the nothingness now inscribed upon our lives
as part of *this* departure.

The Past

That it was never quite like this can never lessen
its infinite appeal; as it recedes
the brighter seems its glory, as the sun
in its late westering offers up
a plenitude of splendours: nondescript
cloud-continents and scattered archipelagos
take on the blazonry of empire, just as if
some imperial monarch had determined
to invest them with the wealth which previously
he had withheld from them...
                            So, too, the past, at times,
shines all the more resplendently the more
it is a gratuitous visitation prompted by
some impulse in the present that suggests
we can live there once more, beyond the unrehearsed
haphazards of the daily world where things
make way for things and nothing is
as it should be were this play merely scripted
to satisfy each ego's audience.

Among the 'Ifs'

If the grave's gate were undone
You would not know your little son...
John Masefield, 'C.L.M.'

But then, you, too, all of you,
would surely come in a different guise:
not in the solemn, sad, ghostly, or shocking
investiture of departure but with some moment
                                                especially chosen
from the lived life, a joyously characteristic and
                                                memorable occasion:
singing around the piano, holding a child for the first time,
receiving a long-awaited letter, digging potatoes, marvelling
at the modest glory of fruit, or the work of Cézanne,
sailing or swimming, the body extending itself
in one of the infinite manifestations of the spirit,
and *that* would be each of you
in the throes of self-forgetfulness
which is at the same time the epitome of oneself
and then our going out would be as nothing,
to our return to the old house
with the kelpie called Ginger there again on the front porch
in that sun-blessed day
as a foretaste of all days to come.

Accountancy

Mother of all mothers, you
Knew what so many mothers knew:
When the time came, your oldest son
Put aside the work he's done
With plane and saw and polished wood
And signed up for the common good
(For which he'd often spoken).
                                        Then,
Confronted by the kind of men
(Who wait somewhere down every street
Where the pious and the powerful meet),
Was handed over, beaten, stripped,
Of all except his honour, whipped
And mocked (just like, they say,
Such things are even done today
In places such as Gitmo Bay
And many another pleasant spot,
Whether we like to think so, or not).

This universal law abides:
The coin of life has just two sides:
One side is love, the other, loss,
Though many auditors fail to agree
That this is our basic currency.

Invisible Dreaming

When we are *there* it's everything:
Every teacher is thrust into a wooden desk.
Notes are passed around which are incomprehensible.
There are sniggers, and spit-balls, and paper aeroplanes
                              one cannot ever return
Since we are not always sure who threw them.
There are lessons to be learned here,
But there is a sense that we are being hurried, hurried,
And that time is running out: if only we had studied
Seriously when we had the chance! Now it is too late,
And we know that when the bell rings and we waken
It will be too late to go back (it always *is*).

So, here we are in the morning again, with clothes on,
                              smiling vaguely,
As if, in this after-world, we have become
Suddenly clever. Whereas, we know that this is not so,
And that, tonight, when the invisible bell rings again,
We will be thrown back, willy-nilly, into another classroom
As mysterious and inescapable as our first...

The Visitors

after another major operation

Speaking strictly *ex-catheter* of course,
there's nothing quite like the surgical gown,
            the oxygen clip and the IV anti-biotics
to bring in this whole swarming tribe
of bug-eyed hobgoblins to sit by your raised
hospital bed, all completely oblivious of
the public visiting-hours.

How deftly we're translated from that suddenly distant
world to this other where, whatever the circumspection
of our presence, we're run on inescapable rails.
                                        Meanwhile,
it's still with some relief we note that that most
shabby and uncouth of all our visitors turns away
and sadly murmuring say:
'I'm sorry, but next time I *may*
just have to make it a *much longer* stay.'

Swarming!

for the Sydney Swans AFL team

Like bees that buzz around a source of sweetness,
See how they swarm organically round the ball!
They merge by instinct (the fruit of hours of training)
Backing each other up, tirelessly, one and all,
To seize, pass, punch, and kick that leathery attraction,
Tackling the opposition with such glee
You'd swear they'd smuggled on field at least a hundred,
So busy are they, everywhere you can see!

These aren't the largest footie bees you'll encounter,
Nor the ones who fill the wintry sky with 'stars',
But putting them all together in their guernseys,
They'll outshine other teams' particulars,
And, like their namesake swans, you mightn't notice
The invisible power that speeds them on their way.
Thus, underestimated often, they'll surprise you
With the goals they've racked up at the close of play...

All in the Timing

an Aussie Olympics fan voices his opinion

well at least he could have spared us those tears
at the end I mean he knew the distance didn't he
and he wasn't the first by a long shot
to end up on a wooden cross let's face it
he'd been over it often enough the hopes
of the whole nation were on him when he was chosen
for the 'biggie' I mean you'd have thought
he'd pull out all stops to honour our expectations
I mean this was what his whole life was about
wasn't it he said so himself often enough in those
public appearances but then when the big moment came
he just couldn't pull it off could he? He was supposed
to be the world's best right? up there on the starting blocks
going for gold and then hullo he couldn't crack it
I mean to say it's all in the timing surely and if it was
up to me I'd sack that coach for a start
and if they don't you won't find me
hanging around next time and that's a fact.

Singing Hymns

Hymns are the special garments of the soul,
Our body's heavenly raiment;
Such heightened joy and sorrow make us whole,
And are a debt's full payment.

Behold, how lovely is that frequent sight
And sound of folk united in sung prayer,
With voices raised and eyes alight
Surely Our Lord is there,

And leads us now, as He has led
Us loyally for the last two thousand years
To break with Him that blessed unleavened bread
And share His love and tears.

Those songs He sang there in that upper room
Were of blessing, thanks, and praise,
His life is woven on the wide world's loom
Until the end of days.

Sea of Troubles

on the most recent deaths at sea of asylum-seekers

Their deaths spell out the living desperation
that drove these families' decision to embark
in an unseaworthy boat in a foreign land;
the dangers of their daily navigation
of hazards on land drove them finally to the stark
option of those other seas that stand
offering, it seemed, access to hope,
the risks at last seemed simply worth the taking,
but somewhere between there and the alien shore
the ocean took its toll... Elsewhere, we grope
for answers in a land where the frequent aching
lament of the bereaved is used to score
points for this policy or that; but who (this far
from that other *inland* ocean of distrust,
danger, and oppression) now can weigh
more accurately for the homeless each particular
factor which finally drove them to 'We must'
on one especially vulnerable day?

The Singing of Birds

the time of the singing of birds is come
The Song of Songs

Suddenly I was living in this forest
with a continual chorus of singing and twittering
birds; not the quarrelsome kind like lorikeets
discussing domestic issues at nightfall
in the trees in town, but a much happier background
of music which at first I thought was obvious
to everybody; but my family were amused
and unbelieving, and then I
discovered that this modest arrangement
accompanied me wherever I went. I live
in a quiet suburb where only the mumble of passing cars
intrudes, a suburb over which flocks of birds
do fly (mallards, seagulls, ibis).
                              But no, *this*
was my own private orchestra whose notes
followed me everywhere as an accompaniment
to whatever else is going on...
There may be a medical name for it,
but, if so, I don't particularly want to know it.
This bit of the mysterious forest is mine.

You

for Liz

You gave me life again
   After such loss,
Life also with some pain
   -ful bridges to cross...

So, when I see your hand
   Now recreate
Our garden, I understand
   In what poorer state

My world would otherwise
   Have languished too,
If by some blest surmise
   I'd not found you...

All of the caring words
   I've failed to say
Stir in my heart, as early birds
   Long for the day.

Mutuality

We see with each other's eyes and hearts
from when the very seeing starts.
Who knows how much in that first room
before our birth we learn from whom
we take in tremulous insights there,
before being delivered to the air
each then wide-eyed, wide-hearted drawn
to wider vistas in being born?
We, in the time vouchsafed may see
(thanks to the blessed minstrelsy
of caring souls) how music flows
into our widening world: the rose,
tree, hill, all creatureliness
which moves around, above, beneath,
that swims and breathes on us its breath.
Thus, *if* fortunate, we can
thank those lucky stars that ran
across our hearts and minds each day
since first, through that mysterious Milky Way,
we voyaged to this present place
and smiled upon its curious face.

Thanks, Jack!

for my father-in-law, John Chambers

Some think that Art is just the *Mona Lisa*,
Michelangelo's Adam (or some other geezer)
But many of us know better: artistry
Takes *many* forms, is just as likely to be
Found in a builder's work, or in a table
– To each his own as well as he is able!
Each adds its worth to what was there before...

I've got a tool-shed, where with hammer and saw
And nails and plane, you built me two new benches
More beautiful to me than Titian's wenches
– Sturdy and smooth, I've gone out many a day
To look at them, as if they're on display
In some posh gallery... They hold with pride
Whatever bags of fertilizers we provide,
Plus the usual assortment of odds and ends
(Your carpentry has made such things my friends!).
This *added* thanks just needed to be said
For bringing your sound art to enhance our shed!

The Itch

At first it's no more than
a hitched eye-brow a passing pursing
of those unseen lips
beneath the skin while you valiantly
attempt to forget (i.e., resist) that subversive
appeal which your imagination feeds on as you
try to move on while your fingers
treacherously twitch as they remember
other times when they also toyed with the
surrendering impulse: first touching stroking
then ultimately tearing at the proffered
body your mind now spinning with
guilty delight crying at last yes yes yes as you
tear at the inflamed flesh your desire in free-fall
until satiated the damage done the recovery process
set back immeasurably your hands
fall away from the newly-torn bleeding
skin of your world which could also be an intolerable
eczema called war love or any other relevant obsession.

The Wallet

for Andrew Court

Time hath, my lord, a wallet at his back,
Wherein he puts alms for oblivion...
Shakespeare, *Troilus and Cressida*

Sometimes, it may be years, it may be less,
a life is merged with yours and then moves on,
but where and how and why may not be known
until much later word comes back
from that far universe as from a star,
and suddenly you're shaken with this sense
that certain lives which once were most
immediate to yours have lived and gone
and you have only lately learned
something of how they lived, that precious knowledge
coined in a realm whose currency
is rarely any longer recognized
as legal tender, those worn coins
of memory you can never trade
or spend for what they're worth while still
aware of your own penury.

To a Notable Literary Archaeologist

for Dennis, after rereading *Attuned to Alien Moonlight*

You have given me back my poetry.
As the BBC's *Time Team* puts together
Roman mosaics lost under some English field,
so, with your trowel, pick and shovel,
and (most of all) careful final brushwork.
You bring me again (as I read) those possibilities
I had forgotten.

Thank you for returning to me, as well,
their history and context, both of which I,
(being an ahistorical Iron Age survivor)
had no idea still slept there under the green grass.

Past, present, future

*We love the colours and the sheen that call to mind
the past that made them.*

Tanizaki Junichiro

Years ago, when Liz and I first married
we'd often meet in the Japanese gardens,
the most romantic setting here on campus
appropriate to our new landscape of love.
There, the pensive sheen of time would take us in,
the eternal questing of those circular paths,
the carefully cultivated *bonsai* to remind us
art is multi-dimensional after all,
as is human love, and while the world at large
would have us still believe the luckiest love
foredoomed, in respectful patterning of such gardens
there is a peace which is its own reward.
Waters here, bridged by modest red,
speak in their stillness, as also
those polished stones which add their steps
to heaven, while running streams
lyricise the hearts of those who meet
beyond tutorials and the lecture-rooms...

Knitting

for Enid and Nola

Your lives are woollen pullovers you are forever knitting;
even when the particular garment is laid aside
the deft needles of your concern
are still engaged...
                    I've watched you knitting
the 'ravelled sleeve' of other people's cares
on a daily basis, working still from patterns
as venerable as the earth...
                            Behind the mileage of
your constant visiting I hear needles clicking
as you bring the jackets, sweaters, beanies,
of your warmth to those shivering in the chill
winds of circumstance. Even in sleep
the work goes on: *knit one, purl one* into infinity...
The local Guardian Pharmacy displays the colorful comfort
of neighbourhood women's knitting – and much survives
by the wealth of just such lovingly knitted lives.

A Long Way from Stanislavsky

First year at uni and the bank manager on campus
was continually reminding me of my overdraft,
and my friend Barry, also in first year, had got a holiday job
raking up leaves at a handicapped children's home in Hawthorn
but didn't feel like starting it, him still living at home, while I
had a rented room in Carlton. So we agreed: I would go as 'Barry', right?
But after a few days Barry decided he could do with some
spare cash for Christmas, especially having learnt the work
was not exactly back-breaking... So I said to him: 'Well, I'm sorry,
I'm already 'Barry', so you'll have to go as 'Bruce'. Okay?'

So there we were, raking up the leaves in our old clothes
and our new identities. Of course,
I had to remember I was the ex-Christian Brothers football star,
cricketer, and so on, and *he* had to remember to be the uni-student poet
living in a room in Carlton. So, every so often I'd ask Barry
how the poetry was going, and he'd drawl something casual about
still knocking out the odd sonnet; then he'd remember to ask me
something about upcoming matches, team problems, etc.

There were other young blokes also raking up leaves
and it still took the two of us a while to get our altered egos
straight, including sometimes having to stress our new names
to each other when we forgot (like '*Barry*...' or '*Bruce*...').
And now and again this was compounded by some young bloke
who'd vaguely known Barry *before* (at school perhaps) and who'd mutter
'It's funny, Bruce, but I keep on wanting to call you 'Barry'!'
To which Barry (*soi-disant* Bruce) would respond, leaning
on his rake: 'Yeah, well, those things happen, mate.'

So, whenever I read about spies assuming new identities, and the intensive training they get before being sent out on their missions, I think of me and Barry and the double-takes we had to do daily.

Beyondness

Though earthly bound by words and flesh,
continually we seek to fly
to where this world and elsewhere mesh
and there is amplitude of sky.

Beyond the lifetime of each day
we hunger for more lasting bread
and would, if we could have our way,
realise that endless meal instead.

Heart, soul, intellect, seem to know
of nourishment (denied us still)
in dreams and visions here below
our mortal hungering would fulfil...

Akin to those migrating birds
which fly from north and south each year;
however feathered, our best words
are fettered to this hemisphere,

and bear the mortal shape which will
mark out our passage and those scars
which link us to the stony hill,
our boomerangs aimed at the stars.

The Me and the You

If you happen to have two different editions of the same book
I will choose to read the older one, preferably,
with yellowing pages and vulnerable binding
– since the older one says, 'When you're reading *me*
you're reading the younger *you*,
the one you hung onto when you had a brighter *me*
to think upon, the way you go back to any old place
and find something there that the present
just hasn't got, since the *you* looking out from that window
is a different younger *you* and we both know
that despite the journeying we've both taken to *now*,
you kept faith with your memories of *then*,
like old friends who were (and are) irreplaceable, and so
we lean out of such windows out of respect
for that ageing schoolmaster, the *past*,
still waving to *us* from wherever he happens to be...'

(Then)

The way it *was* is never the way it was,
anymore than we are ever the way we were;
the present (that passing breeze) winks as it goes,
just as the clouds that shadow us, too, aver
the transient nature of all enterprise.

Could we return to *then*, it would surprise
us somewhat, in how much its very self
differs from what we thought (in future) it was,
having constructed it noiselessly in order
to make it more acceptably suitable

to our continuing *creaturely* wish to be
possessed of what it means as, moving on,
we seek for a future which will, one way or another,
reassure us, just as the furniture, scratched or shining,
in the back of the moving van is murmuring still:

'There, there, all is not lost, these things
(chairs, table, favourite battered books)
for better, for worse, for many things hard to recall,
but insistently just the same, in the back of our hearts,
will offer their needful fictions beyond all facts.'

Epidermis

Consider the world as an epidermis:
an organ holding together those fractious parts
which ideally should work together for
the benefit of the whole,
just as we, individually (or whatever the term is)
limbs, torso, lungs, liver, head, heart –
exist so often in a state of war,
and find ourselves, body and soul,
torn between acceptance of inherent limitations
(reflected in those historical charts we find
hung on each bed), while each nation's
special itches are there to remind
us how pleasurable it would immediately be
to scratch such sources of irritation for the intense relief
such violent action offers – only later to see
how torn and bloodied skin adds to our present grief.

A Question

Some years ago, across our next-door neighbour's driveway
we had another neighbour who, unlike the present one, did occasionally
speak to us, and one day I was over at our side- fence passing the time of day
in the usual inconsequential manner when out of the blue
she suddenly said, 'Do you fellowship?!'

I must have muttered something inconsequential in return
startled as I was by her question because I can't recall
speaking to her again before she and her family left.

But that question still hangs in the air like smoke
after a grass-fire and not at the time being quick enough
on the uptake I'm left wondering just what would have happened
if I'd said 'Yes' or 'Certainly'.

Like a Masonic handshake that special question
often has me pondering, since I've never really seen myself
as a fellowship person so perhaps it was *her* longing
for a fellow she might ship on within a neighbourhood
where there aren't too many 'Hello' or 'Welcome' signs
being run up the main-mast.

But then of course the unexpected is a natural part
of the ocean on which we sail as the frequent FOR SALE signs
around here remind us, so I keep on wondering still
just why I'm wondering.

Sailors

Sailors who have never seen the sea
whose oceans are the scrubby hills, the plains,
whose tidal fortunes, wealth or poverty,
depended upon fair winds and temperate rains.

Sailors whose tricky decks are slippery streets
and board-rooms where the boom becomes the bust
whose lanyards each executive coolly greets
and weather-wise learns hardly who to trust.

Sailors from the factory and the pit
where machinery in one fell swoop could drown
a hundred in a pitiless wave when it,
driven by unseen forces takes them down.

Sailors who every day when skies are blue
on roads find just how vulnerable they are,
the pleasant breezes with satiric cue
mocking the ambos and the bloody car.

Sailors who having served before the mast
of life and country, it's awful burdens bearing,
now marching with slower steps than in the past
whose final uniform's the weariness they're wearing.

A Voice from Limbo

for Lucy Sullivan, author of *False Promises* (2012), which deals with the increase in violence and crime since the 1960s

Long past the middle ages of *my* life
I've found myself, too, in a darkening wood,
complaining often, to my second wife,

who, like Dante's Virgil, comforts (as she should)
but, being much younger and by strong faith bound,
is considerably less dismayed; she even could

(were I listening, for once) expound
how I got there. All I could see
was, as your book spells out, that most profound

and threatening universe which was, for me,
extending its miasma until now,
with no end in sight; the unequivocal Tree

submerged in a drug-laden undergrowth, many a bough
twined round with soporific vines, the young
too often sprawled, or brawling, or somehow

crime-driven, wasted. What sweet singers sung
these many to the circles of their Hell?
What predators have doomed them to eat dung?

What Lions, Leopards, and what She-Wolves wait
to seize these stumbling victims, and what grief
lies in the darkening tempo of their fate?

What governmental wisdoms brought relief
from those false friends who everywhere relate
their burgeoning business to each wrecking reef?

Ah, Lucy, may your vision continue to tell
the plangent history of our post-war world
when too few of those suffering here can spell

the dangers that it holds, may you, too,
like Dante's Beatrice, inspire in turn,
others to tell the bogus from the true

and the warming flames from the consuming fire!

A New Dawn's Arisin'

Thanks to the glossary in *Morte d'Arthur* and my son Brian
(who passed it on to me)
I have learnt that in Middle English our family name
meant 'to dawn; to awaken, revive.' Already this knowledge
has been a source of such enlightenment that I have become
a much more forward-looking verb, and the alternative noun
mere foolishness. Encouraged by this widening sense
of an ancestral present which now like sunrise
reaches back into a past where antecedents are standing
proudly, arms spread in an ever-widening gesture,
while the darkness shrouding their history beyond Dorset
is in full retreat before the all-encompassing
and revivifying sight of that monosyllabic name,
as others seek blessing from convict predecessors,
from hyphenated significancies
or distantly royal history. Like them this knowledge
brings alive the glowing beatitude of the past,
ensuring that in future I will become
even more insufferable than I already am.

Like a Child

During the night I heard this old black dog
crying like a child. Liz had found him
wandering the streets like all the others
she has rescued. But he was really old
and almost totally blind, with white eyebrows
and a boxer's blunt head and he was missing
his home just as much as if he were human.
Every so often through the night
he whimpered in his confusion and bitter
sense of loss of what was especially dear to him.
In the morning he kept coming back to muzzle up to me
for patting and we only hoped the local refuge
for old and infirm animals would take him in,
but we feared it was too late for him to make
new friends in this exquisitely incomprehensible
new world. So we learn again what 'haunted' means.

Present Continuous Santa?

I saw Santa in the street again this Easter
(Reindeer, red suit, and (of course), the sleigh).
He looked a little weary (and at least a
Little out-of-sorts...). I heard him say:

'Once upon a time, the Christmas season
Had a particular beginning, *and*– an end;
Nowadays it seems, for some odd reason,
Those supermarket blokes aim to extend

My special *niche*, so now I find I'm battling
Bunnies and baskets of little chocolate eggs,
While those poor reindeer also find, these rattling
Present times, they're quite run off their legs!

There's just no let-up now; in January
Hot-cross buns are everywhere on sale
– Whatever else they *once* meant, now their very
Existence *all year round* tells you the tale!'

For Ken Goodwin

You were a friend whose kindness knew no limit,
who, if I'd never had a friend before,
would have made friendship worth a world of seeking
and had this seeker knocking at every door...
There are, in every lifetime special people,
and you have always been just such a one
whose instant magnanimity (times without number)
included me as warmly as the sun
shines on a wheat-field which, when nearing harvest,
would (if it could) bow down to the golden west
– as one of the many wheatstalks you've encouraged
you were a full sheaf to my life-long quest.

Genesis Revised

Suppose, (we'll say), a snake, suitably dressed
and equipped with qualifications as a man,
were to be detected, finally
for what he was, those tell-tale scales
gleaming in a sudden patch of sunlight
– what would the authorities at Elysium High
decide upon? The full heel of the law
and what would follow: public obloquy
rebounding on a school which, previously,
the world at large had always taken to be
another reconstructed paradise? And how many
Adams, tempted like the first
to smother the transgression, would begin
enquiring if there might just be an opening
elsewhere to permit the snake to vanish
from what were else a model garden-plot,
enabling all to shake their sorry heads
if, as would seem likely, the same creature
should commit a similar offence at Terra High?

Mersey Valley Cheese

a love poem

You cry out to me like a remembered love;
between our meetings I am mindful of your dear flavour,
your tang your sharp taste so far above
all others. There is that savour
so memorable (although I am the first to admit
I'm no connoisseur of cheeses)
but ever since our first meeting (it
seems like yesterday) it pleases
me to believe our relationship is timeless,
and yet here I am still in this secret world
where the palate of love should be rhymeless
like a young surfer confronting the call
and swell of the limitless ocean.
I have no wish to know what particular sweet
cattle you came from nor in what cool churn (and so
on) you languished until anticipating your swain's devotion
dressed for the market you made your languid way
here to my thankful table
solicitous as that firm of solicitors: Ready, Willing & Able.

From the Parapets

Each of us, over time, becomes acquainted
with the universal war in which we fight,
by future, past, or present onslaughts haunted
(sometimes particular enemies compete...).

Battlefields for many are carefully hidden;
wounds of all kinds affect our very being;
both old and young may often find a sudden
land-mine at their feet has just been sprung.

From conception we're conscripted soldiers, wearing
uniforms in life's lottery, soon or late;
there is no neutral zone to which those fearing
the lot of common soldiers may retreat.

Trench-bound, we are constantly reminded
of the stretcher-bearers who, in many ways
often under fire, bring in the wounded;
a sight to gladden even shell-shocked eyes.

The crosses in war cemeteries still remind us
of all who shouldered arms for good or ill,
may we, whatever darknesses surround us,
choose earthworks which may prove defensible,

And, from our parapets, perceive the danger
which no-man's-land presents to all who live,
and honour those whose ever-present hunger,
like that of stretch-bearers, is to save.

Change and Emily Dickinson

an end-of-year poem for my U3A friends

And if I ever change my mind
About a book to set
For study, which I am inclined
(Temporarily) to regret,

I tell myself that life is short
However long it be
And so, forever being taught,
I *should* just wait and see

Ah, well, Emily you would say
(With those wide, knowing eyes)
Time in its parental way
May yet spring a surprise,

And, smiling in its elfin style,
Decide the choice was just
– Thus does many a quiet smile
Auger again your trust...

Gallipoli

Tread lightly, where so many bled
For little earthly gain;
This was our 'bloody Omaha':
Eight months of bitter pain.

Unfavourable weather, other delays
Blurred the plan of attack...
Landing, the hills confronted them,
The Aegean Sea at their back.

Remember Hill 971,
Lone Pine, and Chunuk Bair?
How often did our records state,
'Another close-fought affair'!

Nations may choose shaping events
By victories which they've had:
Salamis, for ancient Greece,
For Russia, Stalingrad.

And many another nation learns,
In its own ineluctable school:
Turkey remembers its nationhood, too,
Freed from Ottoman rule.

Yet Gallipoli is that victory
Which not all nations greet
– A shining paradox which finds
Affirmation in defeat.

In that same landscape presently
Thousands in peace will trace
The lineaments of those battlefields,
And many a tear-stained face

Pay tribute to Anzac valour
That served to define us, too,
With the dogged sun of their courage
Above that sea of blue.

The Girl from Dalby

for my late wife, Gloria, and for St Saviour's College

About 70 years ago,
back in the days when books
often had document-thick pages,
your friends in Dalby gave you
Dorita Fairlie Bruce's *That Boarding School Girl*,
with their dedication: 'To Dear Dooley
With Love From
Lila Joan and Shirley xxx.'
It's a finely-told tale about a quest for unity
between two schools which had a long tradition
of unfriendliness. Reading it drew me into
a different world with its own language,
and particular concerns,
(with the help of the boarding-school girl,
the long-term school problems were finally
resolved, to everybody's considerable satisfaction).
Gloria, remembering you as I read it,
I thought of your own spirited presence,
both at 7 Stores Depot where I first met you,
and of your fondness for *St Saviour's*...
Turning those pages, your book became
a treasured artefact, like a Sumerian
brick tablet from Nineveh, the cuneiform
become a uniform, and all those
millennia become moments.

www.ingramcontent.com/pod-product-compliance
Lightning Source LLC
Chambersburg PA
CBHW020212090426
42734CB00008B/1041